Cherish

Cherish

THE ONE WORD THAT CHANGES
EVERYTHING FOR YOUR MARRIAGE

STUDY GUIDE
SIX SESSIONS

GARY THOMAS

WITH BETH GRAYBILL

ZONDERVAN®

ZONDERVAN

Cherish Study Guide
Copyright © 2017 by Gary Thomas

This title is also available as a Zondervan ebook.

Requests for information should be addressed to:
Zondervan, *3900 Sparks Dr. SE, Grand Rapids, Michigan 49546*

ISBN 978-0-310-08073-2

Cover design: James W. Hall IV
Interior design: Denise Froehlich

First Printing November 2016 / Printed in the United States of America

HB 01.25.2024

Contents

Introduction

Whether you were married inside a beautiful church, a spectacular event space, the local fire hall, or outside in a country meadow, one thing you share with your group members is that you exchanged some version of wedding vows on that special day. You may have written your own vows that you crafted and carefully designed to reflect your unique personalities. Or you may have said more traditional vows that went something like this:

> I take you to be my wedded husband/wife,
> To have and to hold, from this day forward,
> For better, for worse, for richer, for poorer,
> In sickness and in health,
> To love and to cherish, till death do us part,
> According to God's holy ordinance;
> Therefore I pledge myself to you.

Millions of married couples have repeated these same vows year after year, ceremony after ceremony. In fact, the oldest version of these traditional marriage vows can be traced all the way back to the medieval era. In 1549, these vows were printed in the first Book of Common Prayer that was used by the Church of England.

Today, as Christians, we often revisit these vows when we talk about what it means to *love* our spouses. In fact, most marriage books challenge us to explore a biblical view of *love*. But how often do we stop to think about what it means to *cherish* one another? In this study, you will explore the biblical view of what it means to *cherish*. You will be challenged to take your love to a new level—an "upstairs" level, as one writer puts it—by learning what it means to truly *cherish* your spouse.

My perspective, after years of marriage ministry, is this: *Love is the athletics of marriage, and cherish is the ballet of marriage.* Cherish introduces us to *artistry* in a way that love introduces us to *endurance*. We cannot cherish our spouse without love, and we cannot take our love to a new level without cherishing one another. Studying how to cherish one another, with all its special qualities, puts a polish on love, makes it shine, and adds a special sparkle to our lives and marriages.

Together, during the next six sessions, we will explore the differences between loving and cherishing and take a deeper look at what it means to continue cherishing our spouse "till death do us part."

How to Use This Guide

〜〜

The *Cherish* curriculum is designed to be as personal as is it practical. Each session begins with an opening "icebreaker" question followed by a reflection from the Bible. You will then watch the video with your group and jump into some directed small group discussion. Note that even though there are multiple questions and activities available for your small group, you don't need to feel as if you must use them all. Your leaders will focus on the ones that resonate most with your unique group and guide you from there.

The final component of each session, the *group activity*, is where *Cherish* might diverge from other studies you have done in the past. In this part, each couple will engage in a hands-on exercise that will seek to move the focus of the session from your head to your heart. Think of this time as an answer to the question, "What am I supposed to *do* with this message?"

The group activity is intended to be completed during your meeting time—and it will be what you make of it. If you choose to only go through the motions, or if you refrain from participating with your spouse, it will be less likely you will find what you're looking for during this study. But if you stay open and take a gamble, you may discover what so many others have already found to be true: faith comes alive when we take holy risks for God.

Now, if the thought of *risky* activities make you feel anxious, that's okay. If you fall into this category, just read ahead to each group activity section, and you will know not only what's coming up but also how to prepare yourself accordingly. Finally, remember that none of these exercises or experiences involves anything inappropriate or embarrassing. They are just hands-on opportunities to keep you open to God's love and help you learn to cherish your spouse.

Following your group time, there will be three more opportunities during the week for you to engage the content of *Cherish*. Each of the between-sessions activities is based on the understanding of what it means to cherish and be cherished. A complete understanding of this concept includes recognizing how you want to be cherished, how best to cherish your spouse, and how God has cherished you. The challenge is to do at least one of these activities between sessions and to *use this study guide to record what you learn*.

Starting in session 2, there will be time before the video for you to check in about the previous week's activity and process your experiences as a group. Note that if you could not do an activity the first week, or if you are just joining the study at this point, you don't need to worry. Just hearing what others have learned will be enough at this stage.

Finally, remember that this study represents an opportunity to discover a new way of relating to your spouse. The videos, discussions, and activities are simply meant to kick-start your imagination so that you are not only open to God's love but also start letting it change you from the inside out. Just consider what God could do with a group of people who were not only cherishing their spouses but also cherishing one another together in biblical community. Let's jump into *Cherish* and find out.

Note

If you are a group leader, additional instructions and resources for leading the group activities are included in the back of this book. Because some of the activities require materials and setup, make sure to read this information before the session begins so you will be prepared.

To Love and to Cherish

Love is the muscle of marriage.
Cherish is the heart of marriage.

GARY THOMAS

"*To love and to cherish . . . till death do us part.*" How many of us said these vows on the day we were married? Whether we spoke with a nervous, shaky voice or a confident, exuberant promise, most of us—if not all of us—said something to this effect on that special day at the altar. Since then, we might have read marriage books, gone through couples studies or couples counseling, and perhaps had numerous conversations about what it means to love one another. But rarely do we talk about what it means to cherish one another.

To *cherish* something means to protect it, respect it, notice it, honor it, show gratitude for it, and hold it dear. Think about this for a moment. If you had a Tiffany engagement ring, would you put it in a shoebox? If you had a painting by Rembrandt, would you place it in a Popsicle stick frame? If you had an autographed document from George Washington, would you use it as a coaster? (If you *would* do these things . . . well, that's for a different study.)

When we *cherish* something, we put energy into showcasing it and protecting it. The same is true of marriage. When we cherish our spouses—as opposed to just *loving* our spouses—we strengthen, enrich, and deepen our relationships. We take our marriages to the "upstairs level" of living—the level where we are the truest versions of ourselves, feel most comfortable to see and be seen, and are our most authentic, honest, and real.

Of all the metaphors that could be used to describe cherishing in marriage, perhaps the best is what happens in a ballet. In the *pas de deux* of ballet—the couples' dancing—the male dancer showcases the beauty, grace, strength, and coordination of his partner, the female dancer. It's the dance behind the dance. It's the intentional, meaningful, and purposeful choice of the male dancer to showcase the female. In doing so, the male supports and stabilizes the female as she lifts and turns, allowing her to perform feats she could never do alone.

In this first session, we will examine how marriage really takes off when we get some of our highest pleasure from seeing others honor, appreciate, and admire our spouse. This is one step above even selflessness. We're not merely serving; we're showcasing. That changes our heart toward our spouse and makes him or her feel even more cherished. And cherished spouses tend to thrive more than those who believe they are a colossal disappointment or embarrassment to the other person.

Let's get started.

Welcome and Checking In

Go around the group and invite the members to introduce themselves, and then discuss the following questions:

- How did you meet your spouse?
- What stands out to you from your wedding day?
- What are you hoping to get out of this time together as an individual, as a couple, and as a group?

Take a few moments to share your expectations with the group.

Watch the Video

Play the video segment for session one. As you watch, use the following outline to record any thoughts or concepts that stand out to you.

Notes

Love is the athletics of marriage, but *cherish* is the ballet— the wonder, the art, the mesmerizing aspect of romance. Cherish provides the artistry in marriage.

Ballet is woman, and all my life I
have dedicated my art to her.

GEORGE BALANCHINE

Some of the differences we find in the Bible between *love* and *cherish:*

LOVE (1 Corinthians 13)	CHERISH (Song of Songs)

Wives want to be more than *loved* by their husbands if you define love as commitment or "hanging in there." Husbands may be uncomfortable with the word *cherish*, but they certainly want the concept of what this means. Cherishing will motivate you to pursue each other.

Rather than having our love diminished by each other's imperfections, we can cherish each other's gifts and showcase our spouse's abilities. As George Balanchine said, "The beautiful becomes yet more beautiful."

Marriages will change for the better when we start to focus on showcasing and supporting the other person.

I believe cherish to be a
higher plan within the context
of love, something like the
upstairs level in a home.

JAN KARON

God uses stories of couples who struggle, persevere, and
come out on the other side. But we also need in the church
today stories of couples who cherish each other—who find
the sweet happy spot of marriage.

We don't want marriages where we just grit our teeth and vow
to tolerate each other because the Bible says we don't qualify
for a divorce. The good news is that we can learn to cherish
one another, even if we've stopped doing this in the past.

Cherishing is not based on infatuation but
authenticity—on knowing someone, preferring someone,
and choosing someone above all others. This is why
cherish can take your marriage to a new place.

Cherish looks at the idealized
form of marriage—how we can
have the type of marriages
that inspire others.

Group Discussion

Take a few minutes with your group members to discuss what you just watched and explore these concepts in Scripture.

1. Before everyone shares in the large group, turn to one or two people next to you and finish this sentence: "After watching the video, one question I now have is . . ."

2. What stands out to you from the video teaching: a story, a quote, a thought, an idea? Explain.

3. Other than your spouse, whom or what do you cherish? How would your spouse answer that question for *you*?

4. Read **1 Corinthians 13** aloud, several volunteers taking turns reading a few verses each. According to this passage, what does it *look* and *feel* like to be loved?

5. Now read **Song of Songs 1** aloud, choosing three volunteer readers for the various "speakers" in the dialogue. According to this passage, what does it *look* and *feel* like to be cherished?

6. When was a moment in your life when you remember being cherished by your spouse, a family member, or a friend? How have you felt cherished by God?

7. Read **Psalm 139:1–18** aloud, again using volunteer readers. What does this passage say about the way God loves us and cherishes us?

8. What is one action step you could take with your spouse as a result of this session?

Group Activity

For this activity, each participant will need a piece of paper and a pen to record ideas.

Part of understanding and exploring what it means to *cherish* one another is verbalizing what it means to be cherished. This may seem simple for some, but for others, it will require thought and maybe a few examples. So, take a few minutes as a couple to talk about *what makes you feel the most cherished by people in your life*. Is it a phone call or a message from a friend during the week? Is it sharing pieces of your story as you relate to another person? Is it spending time together outside of group time or sharing a meal together? When everyone is finished, share your best idea as a couple with the group.

Closing Prayer

Take a few moments to pray together in some of the following directions:

- Ask God to show you ways that he's loved and cherished you as individuals and as couples.
- Ask God to allow this message of how to cherish to sink

deep into your hearts and minds as you seek to deepen your love for your spouse.

- Ask God to show you what it really looks like to cherish your spouse.
- Ask God to open yourselves up to authenticity, honesty, and vulnerability as you spend time together as a group.
- Thank God for his presence in your lives, for the people in your group, and for the opportunity to cherish your spouse in new ways as a result.

Between-Sessions Personal Study

Explore the material you've covered this week by engaging in at least one of the following between-sessions activities. (Some are stand-alone; others are connected to a prior activity.) These activities are meant to provide additional opportunities for you and your spouse to climb the staircase from the "ground floor level" of love to the "upstairs level" of cherish. After doing an activity, be sure to reflect and make a few notes in your guide about the experience.

Day One: Understand Your Spouse

Take a few moments this week to have a conversation with your spouse. Ask your spouse, *"What are some things I do that make you feel cherished?"* When it's your turn to answer, be realistic and be honest. Your spouse cannot read your mind, nor can he or she make all of your dreams come true every day. However, you and your spouse *can* learn to start cherishing each other in ways that will be most meaningful to both of you.

Read **Philippians 1:9–10** as a couple and make it your prayer today: *Lord, I pray that our love will overflow more and more, and that we will keep on growing in knowledge and understanding. We want you to teach us what really matters, so that we may live pure and blameless lives before you until the day of Christ's return.*

Day Two: Cherished by Your Spouse

Based on your answers to the first activity, take a few moments to individually write down two or three ideas about how you could cherish your spouse this week. Then share those ideas with each other. If you've "missed the mark" with your ideas, revisit the first activity, seek to listen to your spouse, and try to better understand how your spouse wants to be cherished.

-

-

-

Read **Ephesians 4:2–3** as a couple and make it your prayer today: *God, we want to always be humble, gentle, and patient with each other. We want to make allowances for each other's faults because of your love. Help us to be mindful of your love for us and your peace that unites our hearts together. Thank you for being with us in our marriage.*

The way we treat something acknowledges
whether we cherish it or hold it with indifference
or contempt. To truly cherish something is to
go out of our way to show it off, protect it, and
honor it. We want others to see and recognize
and affirm the value of what we see.

CHERISH, PAGES 16–17

Day Three: Cherished by God

Think about past moments in life when you felt cherished by God, both as individuals and as a couple. *What was the specific situation? What happened to make you feel cherished? How did that change your life?* Write down those moments, and then share them with each other. Make sure you listen to your spouse without interrupting as he or she shares.

Read **Psalm 139:1–6** as a couple and make it your prayer today: *You have searched us, Lord, and you know us. You know when we sit and when we rise. You perceive our thoughts from afar. You discern our going out and our lying down. You are familiar with all our* *ways. Before a word is on our tongue, you, Lord, know it completely. Thank you for your presence in our marriage and for wonderful understanding that comes only from you.*

Day Four: Cherish in Action

Set aside some time today to take action on one of the ways you previously identified as how your spouse feels most cherished. If possible, cherish your spouse *and* allow your spouse to cherish you in ways that are most meaningful to both of you. Remember, this is about cherishing your spouse, not about being the "kind hero." Take a few moments to journal your thoughts after your cherish activities. Ask yourself: *What was it like to cherish my spouse? What was it like to be cherished? What was difficult about doing this?*

Read **Proverbs 4:8** as a couple and make it your prayer today: *Lord, help us today to cherish your wisdom as we cherish one another. We want to embrace your wisdom so we will honor one another and exalt you in all we say and do toward each other. Continue to show us what it means to cherish, embrace, and honor each another in the days, months, and years ahead.*

> Beautiful, harmonic marriages are like the ballet and symphony. They're not just one dancer or one note. They are built by asking ourselves on a regular basis, "Am I trying to showcase my spouse, or am I fixated on how my spouse is not showcasing me?"
>
> CHERISH, PAGE 49

Day Five: Carrying a Burden

Yesterday, you and your spouse took action on cherishing one another. Today, the goal is to cherish your spouse in a practical way by taking on a task that he or she normally does. Begin by asking each other, "How can I support you today? How can I make your day better? Is there something I can take on for you that would show the way I cherish you?" Write down your spouse's response in the space and how you will address it—and then go do it.

Read **Galatians 6:2** as a couple and make it your prayer today: *Father, today we want to demonstrate our love for you, and for each other, by carrying one another's burdens. Please help us as we continue to grow in understanding of what it means to cherish each other. Thank you for always carrying our burdens when we come to you in prayer.*

Further Reflection

If you would like to dig a bit deeper into the idea of how to cherish your spouse, read chapters 1–3 in the *Cherish* book and reflect on the following questions:

- Which story in these chapters stands out to you most? Why?
- What steps will you take this week to make your spouse feel as if he or she is "the only man or woman in the world"?
- Think about your spouse's unique personality and gifts. What is the best way you can draw on these characteristics to "showcase" your spouse?

Use the space below to write any key points or questions you want to bring to the next group meeting.

Your Honor

If we want to cherish our spouses, then we have to honor them.

GARY THOMAS

How do we show honor to our spouses? Consider the stories of two couples: Sara and Ryan, and Leslie and Connor.

For Sara, baseball wasn't her first idea of spending a fun afternoon together with her husband, Ryan. But their hometown team was playing in Ryan's favorite ballpark, and three of her husband's best childhood friends had tickets too. So, Sara decided it was worth the "sacrifice" to go to the game. The couple found their seats just before the game started. Sara had an aisle seat, next to Ryan, followed by a string of his friends.

Every time there was a hard hit or a great play, Sara would jump to her feet to join in the cheering. Ryan would also jump to his feet, but then he would turn to his buddies to exchange high fives and loud cheers. He didn't even notice Sara was on her feet as well, cheering and waiting with her hand up for a high five. Sara, feeling unnoticed, would then quietly sit down.

Occasionally Ryan would give Sara a quick glance and say, "You having fun, honey?" Play after play, inning after inning, Sara's attempt to be a part of the baseball fun went unnoticed. For most of the night she wondered, *Why did I even come to the game?*

Leslie was getting ready for her work party one Friday evening when she caught an uncomfortable look on her husband Connor's face. "Do you need to loosen your tie?" she asked. "You look really uncomfortable." "No," he replied, "I'm just kind of dreading this party tonight. It takes all my energy to think of questions to ask and things to say to your coworkers. I just don't have much in common with them."

Leslie rolled her eyes as if to say *Don't be ridiculous!* "You have nothing to worry about," she said. "I'll be right there with you! And we always find things to talk about with other people when we're together. Let's be a team!" But Connor knew the truth from past experiences: Leslie would start talking about work projects with her cubicle buddies, and Connor would be left running to the food table for her refills and standing awkwardly on the outer edge of Leslie's conversation circles.

In this second session, we will examine how *cherishing* our spouses means honoring them in the most critical moments as well as the most mundane times of life. It means paying attention to their lives as much as we pay attention to our own. We honor our spouses by catching their bids for our attention—by outdoing them with our loving affection, our words, our protection, and our valiant attempts to chase away any feelings of worthlessness or disregard. There is no room for contempt like this in our marriages when we choose to cherish one another. A good marriage is all about honor.

Let's get started.

Welcome and Checking In

Go around the group and invite any new members to introduce them-selves, and then discuss the following questions:

- What stands out to you from last week's session?
- How have you practiced cherishing your spouse?
- What does the word *honor* mean to you?

Take a few moments to share with the group a time in the past when you felt honored.

Watch the Video

Play the video segment for session two. As you watch, use the following outline to record any thoughts or concepts that stand out to you.

Notes

Every pitch counts in baseball *and* in marriage. A "pitch" in marriage occurs when our spouse makes a comment, asks a question, or seeks our attention. The decision to *not* make a play on that pitch is a still a decision—and it has consequences.

Not to make a decision is to make
a decision. Every pitch counts!

We bow and curtsy to the Queen of England. We stand
when the judge enters a courtroom. We applaud for an
incredible performance. And it is key in our marriages
that we catch those special moments to honor our spouse.
Honoring may occur simply by *noticing* our spouse.

Honor is about "catching the bids" or "reacting to the
pitches" of our spouse. If a baseball player reacts well
and hits just 30 percent of the pitches thrown to him, he
will do great in building his career as a hitter. The same
isn't true for us. Studies show we need to catch nearly 90
percent of the bids sent our way if we want a strong and
healthy marriage.

We cherish our spouses when we outdo each another in
showing honor. It is our personal responsibility to cherish
our spouse more than her or she cherishes us.

We determine whether we are a *marriage disaster* or a *marriage master* by how we handle the pitches or the bids between ourselves and our spouse.

> ## Without honor, all the marriage skills one can learn won't work.
>
> DR. JOHN GOTTMAN

We cherish and honor our spouses when we *pay attention*. It's not about what our spouse says but about who is saying it! We have to listen with our eyes as much as we do with our ears—and maintain eye contact with our spouse as he or she speaks to us.

Cherishing our spouse includes recognizing their desire for physical intimacy. We cherish our spouse when we pursue him or her with *desire* and *delight* relationally, emotionally, and physically. In doing so, we release the perfection of beauty in our spouse's life.

The biblical model of cherishing: God the Father cherished Jerusalem, Christ the Son cherished the church, and we are to cherish our spouse.

> Cherishing within a Christian marriage is about releasing that perfection of beauty in our spouse.

Group Discussion

Take a few minutes with your group members to discuss what you just watched and explore these concepts in Scripture.

1. Before everyone shares in the large group, turn to one or two people next to you and finish this sentence: "After watching the video, one question I now have is . . ."

2. What stands out to you from the video teaching: a story, a quote, a thought, an idea? Explain.

3. Other than your spouse, whom or what do you honor? How would your spouse answer that question for *you*?

4. Have a volunteer read **Ezekiel 16:1–5** aloud to the group. According to this passage, what does Jerusalem look like before God honors her and restores her beauty?

5. Have you ever felt dishonored by someone in your life? How did that affect your relationship? How was honor restored in the relationship, if at all?

6. Have two volunteers read **Zechariah 8:1–8** aloud to the group. What does this passage say about the way God will bring honor to Jerusalem?

7. Have another volunteer read **Romans 12:10** aloud to the group. According to this passage, what does it *look* and *feel* like to be honored?

8. What is one action step you could take with your spouse as a result of this session?

Group Activity

For this activity, each participant will need a piece of paper and a pen to record ideas.

Part of understanding and exploring what it means to *cherish* one another is verbalizing what it means to honor and be honored. This may seem simple for some, but for others, it will require thought and maybe a few examples. So, take a few minutes as a couple to talk about *what makes you feel the most honored by people in your life.* Is it the way they listen to you? Is it the way they treat you in public and in private? Is it the way they express a desire to be with you and truly understand you? Is it the way they bring out the best in you? When everyone is finished, share your best idea as a couple with the group.

Closing Prayer

Take a few moments to pray together in some of the following directions:

- Ask God to allow you to forgive those people in your life who have dishonored you.
- Ask God to show you what it really looks like to honor your spouse and, by doing so, also honor him.
- Ask God to open yourselves up to authenticity, honesty, and vulnerability as you spend time together as a group.
- Thank God for his presence in your lives, for the people in your group, and for the opportunity to honor and cherish your spouse in new ways.

Between-Sessions Personal Study

SESSION 2

Explore the material you've covered this week by engaging in at least one of the following between-sessions activities. These activities are meant to provide additional opportunities for you and your spouse to climb the staircase from the "ground floor level" of love to the "upstairs level" of cherish. After doing an activity, be sure to reflect and make a few notes in your guide about the experience.

Day One: Understanding Your Brokenness

Take a few moments this week to have an honest conversation with your spouse. Ask him or her, "How have you felt dishonored in the past—by me or by others?" If your spouse shares something personal with you, listen and ask for forgiveness if you need to do so. Understanding your spouse's brokenness will help you restore honor to your spouse in a meaningful way. Also ask your spouse, "What makes you feel most honored by me?"

When it's your turn to answer these questions, be realistic and be honest. Keep in mind your spouse may not see your brokenness until you share it and may not catch all of your "pitches" or "bids" to be honored every day. However, you and your spouse *can* learn to start honoring and cherishing each other in ways that will be most meaningful to both of you.

Read **Romans 12:10** as a couple and make it your prayer today: *Lord, help us to love each other with genuine affection. Show us what it means to be devoted to each other in love. We want you to teach us to honor you and honor one another more than we honor ourselves.*

Day Two: Honored by Your Spouse

Based on your answers to the first activity, take a few moments to individually write down two or three ideas about how you could honor your spouse this week. Then share those ideas with each other. If you've "missed the mark" with your ideas, revisit the first activity, seek to listen to your spouse, and try to better understand how he or she wants to be honored.

Read **Philippians 2:3–4** as a couple and make it your prayer today: *God, show us how and where we pursue our own selfish ambitions in our marriage. We want to value each other above our own selves. Help us to set aside our own personal interests for the interests of each other as we seek to honor one another. Thank you for leading the way in your example of how to love and honor one other and the world around us.*

A key principle to honoring your spouse is understanding that the person being honored gets to determine how they want to be honored.

CHERISH, PAGE 61

Day Three: Honored by God

Think about reminders from Scripture or past moments in life when you felt honored by God, both as individuals and as a couple. *What was the specific situation or specific reminder? What happened to make you feel honored? How did that change your perspective on life?* Write down those reminders (or moments) and share them with each other. Make sure you listen to your spouse without interrupting as he or she shares.

Read **Psalm 8:1–9** as a couple and make it your prayer today: *Lord, how majestic is your name in all the earth! With all of your glory, you made the heavens and the earth, and you were mindful of us the whole time. Thank you for the way you care for us and for crowning us with glory and honor. Help us to comprehend what this means in our lives and in our marriage as we seek to honor you and honor one another.*

Day Four: Honor in Action

Set aside some time today to take action on one of the ways you previously identified as how your spouse feels most honored. If possible, honor your spouse *and* allow your spouse to honor you in ways that are most meaningful to both of you. Remember, this is about outdoing your spouse with honor, not about being the "best." This means *sharing the lows with empathy* and *celebrating the highs with enthusiasm.* It also means *protecting your spouse.*

Take a few moments to journal your thoughts after you express honor to your spouse. Ask yourself: *What was it like to honor my spouse? How did this honor restore beauty to my spouse? What was it like to be honored? Was there anything difficult about doing this?*

Read **John 12:26** as a couple and make it your prayer today: *Lord, help us understand what it means specifically for us to serve you and follow you as individuals and as a couple. We want to bring honor to your name in everything we do and say, especially in our marriage. Thank you for your promise to honor those who serve you.*

Cherishing requires an eager ear and a strategic tongue. It means maintaining our curiosity. . . . What do you admire about your spouse? What makes you smile when you think about your spouse? *Tell* her. *Tell* him.

CHERISH, PAGES 122, 124–125

Day Five: Releasing Beauty

Yesterday, you and your spouse took action on honoring one another. Today, the goal is to honor your spouse and release his or her beauty in a practical way by giving your spouse time to pursue an interest or passion. Begin by asking each other, "How can I support you today? Is there an interest or passion you would like to pursue with some extra time today? Is there something I can take on for you that would show honor to you?" Write down your spouse's response in the space below and how you will address it—and then go do it.

Read **Colossians 3:18–19** as a couple and make this your prayer today: *Father, show us what it means to submit to one another as we seek to honor each another. Give us a love free of harsh words and unkind thoughts. Give us the confidence and courage to release one another's beauty to the world around us by cherishing and honoring one another. Thank you for restoring our brokenness—from past situations and current relationships—and for giving us the opportunity to love and encourage one another in this season of life. We love you, Lord.*

Further Reflection

If you would like to dig a bit deeper into the idea of how to cherish your spouse, read chapters 4, 5, and 8 in the *Cherish* book and reflect on the following questions:

- Which story in these chapters stands out to you most? Why?
- What steps will you take this week to protect, honor, and thank your spouse without being asked?
- How will you affirm your spouse this week with cherishing and honoring words?

Use the space below to write any key points or questions you want to bring to the next group meeting.

Cherishing Your Unique Spouse

Cherishing is about treating our
spouse as a unique individual.

GARY THOMAS

I think it's fair to say we all long for unique experiences in life.
We live in a day and age when we'd rather rent someone's
home or loft apartment through Airbnb or VRBO than stay at
one of the standard hotel chains. We'd rather catch an Uber ride
around town than rent a car or hail a taxi. We cherish these
unique experiences because they feel special and one of a kind.

What if we viewed our spouses the same way? What if we
cherished the unique and special traits in our spouse instead of
focusing on the things that bother us? What if we took the time
to study our spouses and look carefully at the images of their
lives? What if we made a covenant with our minds and hearts to
cherish our spouse above all others, never comparing our spouse
with others in a negative way, and instead enthusiastically delight

in the way God made our spouse to be? Perhaps we would be reminded of the unique qualities that attracted us to them in the first place. Or maybe we would find something new that we never before noticed.

A woman named Ann was quick to admit that for years she glossed right over her husband's unique qualities. Her husband, Dave, had been a stellar athlete and was an accomplished pastor of a large church. He was a confident man who was successful in both his personal and professional life. The problem was that Ann had become so familiar with his accomplishments that she just assumed that's how all husbands were "supposed to be."

Then one day, Dave shared his honest thoughts on their marriage. "It's been difficult," he said, "because it feels like I've been cheered in every area of life—but then I come home and all I hear is, 'Booo, booo, booo!'" In that moment, Ann realized she had set the bar of expectations so high for her husband that she wasn't fully appreciating the fact that he was special and their lifestyle was not the norm. To cherish Dave, she had to figure out how to affirm her highly successful husband.

Some spouses were hugely "successful" before they married us. Others felt beaten down and ridiculed and suffer from a low self-image. Cherishing in marriage is all about learning to appreciate the particular spouse God has given us and becoming a student of our spouse's personal history. It means seeing God as the amazing creator of our spouse's uniqueness.

Let's get started.

Welcome and Checking In

Begin this session by discussing the following questions as a group:

- What stands out to you from last week's session?
- How have you recently practiced honoring your spouse?
- What does sacrifice mean to you?

Take a few moments to share with the group what you feel are some of your unique strengths or unique areas of interest.

Watch the Video

Play the video segment for session three. As you watch, use the following outline to record any thoughts or concepts that stand out to you.

Notes

In marriage, cherishing is all about learning to appreciate the particular spouse God has given to us. It's about understanding their beauty and letting them be your heart's home.

Cherishing our spouse is all about learning the particulars about that person. It involves throwing away the stereotypes and asking the question, "How do I cherish this unique person that God has made?"

Marriages involve unique
individuals. For this reason, what's
good advice for some marriages
could be terrible advice for others.

Recognizing our spouse's unique qualities calls us back
into the Garden of Eden. It's looking at our spouse as the
only man or woman in the world.

Cherishing our spouse as a unique individual starts as a
prayer—*"Lord, I want to look at my spouse as the only man or
woman in the world."* This becomes a *choice* (how we govern
our minds and hearts) that requires *commitment* on our
part. Eventually, this leads to *satisfaction*.

"My dove, my perfect
one, is the only one."

Song of Songs 6:9

When we view our spouse as our unique "Adam" or "Eve," we allow that person to define what a man or woman is for us. We reset the parameters for contentment in marriage and learn to *cherish* the strengths of our spouse instead of just *tolerating* those strengths.

Viewing our spouse as our unique "Adam" or "Eve" has a huge impact in the bedroom. When we cherish our spouse's unique body and physical needs—and keep our heart for our spouse only—it becomes an expression of the deepest kind of love for that person.

Treating our spouses like the only man or woman in the world means studying them—what they like and don't like, what helps them when they are angry, and what they need when they are sad. Cherishing is built on this kind of particular focus.

We can keep pursuing our spouse because they are always changing. Our pursuit to cherish our spouses keeps our curiosity in that person alive—we re-create the same spark we initially felt when we were dating.

If we choose to cherish our spouse and make him or her supreme in our heart, we will never *want* to stray in our marriage. We will view that person as the only man or woman in the world for us—and this will shape our hearts.

You could be married to the most successful woman or man alive, but if they hear you yelling "booo!" there will still be an ache in their souls.

CHERISH, PAGE 143

Group Discussion

Take a few minutes with your group members to discuss what you just watched and explore these concepts in Scripture.

1. Before everyone shares in the large group, turn to one or two people next to you and finish this sentence: "After watching the video, one question I now have is . . ."

2. What stands out to you from the video teaching: a story, a quote, a thought, an idea? Explain.

3. What is something unique about your spouse? How do you celebrate or cherish this uniqueness in your spouse?

4. Have a volunteer read **Song of Songs 6:9** aloud to the group. According to this passage, what does cherishing your unique spouse look like from a biblical perspective?

5. What are some ways that people fall into a pattern of *tolerating* their spouse's unique strengths rather than *celebrating* those strengths? What part does comparing your spouse to other men or women play in this?

6. Have another volunteer read **1 Samuel 16:7** aloud to the group. What does this passage mean to you in regard to cherishing your spouse? What truly matters in a relationship?

7. How do you *study* your spouse? How will getting to know what your spouse likes or how he or she reacts in certain situations affect your contentment in marriage?

8. Ask a third volunteer to read **Romans 12:2** aloud to the group. How does this passage relate to the idea of cherishing your spouse? How can renewing your mind in Christ affect the way you view your spouse as the only man or only woman in the world?

Group Activity

For this activity, each participant will need a piece of paper and a pen to record ideas.

Part of understanding and exploring what it means to *cherish* one another is verbalizing what it means to appreciate and affirm your spouse as you celebrate their uniqueness in the world. So, as you close today's session, take a few minutes to write down a few things you appreciate and find truly unique about your spouse. In addition, write down a few ways that he or she has made sacrifices for you in the past. Share these items with your spouse. Then, when everyone is finished, share one or two of your answers as a couple with the group.

Closing Prayer

Take a few moments to pray together in some of the following directions:

- Ask God to help you forgive past misunderstandings in your marriage and to desire to appreciate and affirm your spouse.
- Ask God to show you what it really looks like to allow your spouse to redefine *beauty* and *strength*.
- Ask God to give you the commitment and courage to view your spouse as the only man or woman in the world.
- Thank God for his presence in your lives, for the people in your group, and for the opportunity to be on this journey together as you work toward a "Garden of Eden" perspective in your marriages.

Between-Sessions Personal Study

SESSION 3

Explore the material you've covered this week by engaging in at least one of the following between-sessions activities. These activities are meant to provide additional opportunities for you and your spouse to climb the staircase from the "ground floor level" of love to the "upstairs level" of cherish. After doing an activity, be sure to reflect and make a few notes in your guide about the experience.

Day One: Cherishing Your Unique Spouse

Take a few moments this week to have an honest conversation with your spouse. Ask each other, "Do you feel like I see your uniqueness? If so, how do you think I express this awareness? If not, what do you wish I would notice about you?" Remember that the goal is to listen and stay open to what your spouse is saying. Don't get defensive, as this will only push your spouse away. Take turns asking these questions, jot down your thoughts, and then share them with your spouse. Finally, ask what you can do to express your love and appreciation to the other person—to make your spouse feel as if he or she is the only man or only woman in the world.

Read **Psalm 139:14** as a couple and make it your prayer today: *Lord, we praise you because we have each been fearfully and wonderfully made by you—as unique individuals. Your works are wonderful, and we know that full well. May we be mindful of the unique and creative way in which you crafted both of us, as your daughter and as your son. Amen.*

Day Two: Praying for Your Spouse

Cherishing your spouse as a unique individual starts with *prayer.* So begin this time today by writing a prayer for your spouse. If you could pray with intention for your spouse, what would you say to God? What would you say about your own heart, about your desire for your spouse, and about your marriage? Share this prayer with your spouse, and then pray your prayers aloud—with and for one another.

Read **Song of Songs 6:9** as a couple and make it your prayer today: *God, please help us to see each other as the unique one, the perfect one, the only one in our marriage. Give us a love that rises above misunderstanding and contentment, a love of desire and intimacy, a love that honors you and honors one another. Amen.*

A cherishing marriage is built on intimate
understanding, not stereotypical assumptions.

CHERISH, PAGE 140

Day Three: Choosing Your Spouse

Cherishing your spouse as a unique individual starts with a *prayer* and then becomes a *choice*. This is an intentional decision on your part to look past your previous misunderstandings, keep on healing from your past hurts, and choose to see your spouse the way that God sees him or her: as a beautiful, handsome, unique, loved, and cherished man or woman. So today, ask yourself: *What does it look like to choose to see my spouse in this way? What would our marriage look like if we both viewed each other this way?* Write down a few thoughts, and then share some of these insights with your spouse.

Read **Romans 12:2** as a couple and make it your prayer today: *Lord, please give us the strength to not conform to the pattern of this world when it comes to our view on marriage. Transform us as individuals and as a couple through the renewing of our minds. Give us the desire to choose what is right and pleasing in your will as we seek to love and cherish one another. Amen.*

Day Four: The Power of Commitment

Cherishing your spouse as a unique individual starts with a prayer, becomes a choice, and then requires a *commitment*. It involves saying, once again, "I choose you, for better or for worse, till death do us part." Ask what this type of renewed commitment would look like in your relationship. Would it mean having a regular special date night? Would it mean posting special pictures of your spouse around your office to remind you that he or she is the only unique one for you? Share your ideas with your spouse and find a unique way to express your marriage commitment that is meaningful to both of you.

Read **John 13:35** as a couple and make it your prayer today: *God, we know that we represent you in the way we choose to love one another. May our marriage be an example to all of our discipleship and devotion to you. Amen.*

> Our marriages are about more than each other;
> they are about testifying to God's kingdom—a
> mission served in part by recognizing the royal
> place each partner has in that kingdom.
>
> CHERISH, PAGE 176

Day Five: Satisfaction of Marriage

Cherishing your spouse as a unique individual starts with a prayer, becomes a choice, requires a commitment, and then eventually leads to *satisfaction*. Think about the ways you have felt emotionally, relationally, and physically satisfied by your spouse. Now think about how this connection affects you spiritually. *How does satisfaction in your marriage affect your relationship with God? How does your relationship with God affect the satisfaction in your marriage?* Talk about this with your spouse for a few minutes.

Read **1 Peter 2:9** as a couple and make this your prayer today: *Father, we thank you that you have created us and called us to be a chosen people, a royal priesthood, your special possession, so that we may declare your praises. We praise you, God, as the One who called us out of darkness and into the light. May we be reminded that* *you continually call us out of the darkness and into the light in every aspect of our lives, including our marriage. Amen.*

Further Reflection

If you would like to dig a bit deeper into the idea of how to cherish your spouse, read chapter 9 in the *Cherish* book and reflect on the following questions:

- Which story in this chapter stands out to you most? Why?
- What steps will you take this week to celebrate the uniqueness of your spouse?
- How will you re-create the spark of curiosity in your relationship?

Use the space below to write any key points or questions you want to bring to the next group meeting.

This Is How Your Spouse Stumbles

Marriage is the art of learning
how your spouse stumbles and
cherishing them through it.

GARY THOMAS

I knew a married couple who gave enormous amounts of grace and patience to the people in their lives—except when it came to each other. In fact, the wife confessed that her husband once told her, "Honey, you are the nicest person I know . . . to everyone except me." Her response? "Well, you give your best to everyone at work, and then I get the worst of you when you walk in the door every evening." Sound slightly familiar?

My wife, Lisa, and I also deal with frustration toward each other from time to time. Early one morning at our house, I woke up a little later than usual, which meant I was in danger of sitting in traffic in the metropolitan area of Houston. I rushed through my normal morning routine and was headed out the door when

I realized I didn't have my car keys. I quietly checked every spot imaginable—not wanting to wake my wife—and even used the light on my phone to look for the keys in our bedroom.

Finally, Lisa stirred and asked what I was doing. When I told her, she said she had taken my keys the night before when she borrowed my car (because she couldn't find her keys), and then stashed them in her purse. It takes Lisa a little longer to wake up in the morning, so finding her purse and my keys took even more time, adding to what already was an increasingly onerous commute. In that moment I could have gotten angry with Lisa, but I realized that what she had done wasn't intentional. Lisa hadn't intended to make life difficult for me—she knew I was frustrated, she understood why, and she knew the consequences of me leaving the house late that morning. So what good would it have done if I had yelled?

Choosing a graceful response toward Lisa actually gave me freedom to let go of the situation and move on with my day. The same will be true in your marriage. To keep cherishing your spouse, it follows that you must be a good forgiver—a person who is eager to show mercy to others as you have been shown mercy by God. The goal of a cherishing marriage is to know the other person so well that you understand the dark corners and the weak links in one another's personalities—yet still cherish, respect, adore, and move toward each other.

Let's get started.

Welcome and Checking In

Begin this session by discussing the following questions as a group:

- What stands out to you from last week's session?
- How have you recently celebrated the uniqueness of your spouse?
- What is something new you learned about your spouse since session three?

Take a few moments to share your thoughts with the group.

Watch the Video

Play the video segment for session four. As you watch, use the following outline to record any thoughts or concepts that stand out to you.

Notes

If we want to help our spouses when they stumble, we need to have the attitude of a physician rather than a prosecuting attorney. We have to let our spouse know that we cherish them for who they are, and want them to be healed—not punished.

MYTH: A great marriage is based on great compatibility.

<small>GARY THOMAS</small>

It's not *compatibility* that determines whether we're going to have a great marriage or not but how we handle each other's sin.

In order to build a cherishing marriage, we have to have compassion for our spouse in the same manner that Jesus and the apostle Paul had compassion for the sinners around them.

"I urge you to live a life worthy of the calling you have received. Be completely humble and gentle: be patient, bearing with one another in love. Make every effort to keep the unity of the Spirit through the bond of peace."

<small>EPHESIANS 4:1–3</small>

Scripture defines being "holy" in large part by our willingness and ability to gracefully bear the lack of holiness in others.

Practicing holiness means learning to recognize that much of sin was conceived in hurt. It's our job to help our spouse heal—to act as God's representative—but not to punish them.

In order to adopt this attitude, we first have to understand that every spouse has certain bothersome tendencies that *won't change*. There is no "perfect" spouse out there. We must learn to *let go* of these bothersome qualities that will always be present in our spouse. This doesn't mean we excuse or enable blatant sin, but that we are gracious as our spouse grows in Christ.

The second thing we must do is learn to look at the *presence behind the problem*. Our spouses may do things that annoy us, but often this is just part of living with another individual.

The third thing we must understand is that *recovery involves relapse*. We don't excuse immoral behavior, but we recognize the motivation behind it and have the empathetic heart that Scripture requires us to have.

The fourth thing we must do to cherish a spouse who stumbles is to give him or her the *benefit of the doubt*. Often our spouse does not intend to hurt us with their words or actions, and we can choose to believe the best about him or her because we know our spouse's character. *Side note:* Cherishing your spouse when he or she says something stupid means (1) holding off on fantasy conversations, and (2) starting conversations with a question instead of leading with an accusation. One way to do this is to simply say, "Tell me what you were thinking." (But watch your tone with that last one.)

The fifth thing we must do is to recognize that our spouse is royalty. We can't always honor our spouse for their behavior, but we can honor them for their place in the royal priesthood of God's kingdom. Christian marriage is about testifying to God's long-term plan for humanity.

A cherishing attitude is one that says, *I will catch you and I will walk alongside you.*

When your spouse stumbles,
a helpful cool-down thought
is the simple "this is how
my spouse stumbles."

CHERISH, PAGE 164

Group Discussion

Take a few minutes with your group members to discuss what you just watched and explore these concepts in Scripture.

1. Before everyone shares in the large group, turn to one or two people next to you and finish this sentence: "After watching the video, one question I now have is . . ."

2. What stands out to you from the video teaching: a story, a quote, a thought, an idea? Explain.

3. What are some of the ways that you have stumbled as a spouse?

4. Ask a volunteer to read **Ephesians 4:1–3** aloud to the group. What does it mean to be *holy*? What does it mean to *live a life worthy of the calling you have received*?

5. What are a few practical and encouraging ways we can respond to our spouse when he or she has a relapse and stumbles again?

6. Have another volunteer read **Colossians 3:12–14** aloud to the group. What does this passage mean to you in regard to cherishing your spouse even when he or she stumbles or messes up?

7. What are the outstanding character qualities you know to be true about your spouse? How can you keep these character qualities in mind when you're tempted to doubt or judge your spouse?

8. Have a third volunteer read **1 Peter 2:9–10** aloud to the group. What does it mean to be a *royal priesthood*? In what ways can you begin to treat your spouse as a king or queen?

Group Activity

For this activity, each participant will need a piece of paper and a pen to record ideas.

Part of building a cherishing marriage is understanding what it means to respond to your spouse as a physician, not as a prosecuting attorney. So, to conclude this session, take a few minutes to think about times when you've treated your spouse as though you were a prosecuting attorney. Do you need to ask your spouse's forgiveness for those moments? In what areas of life does your spouse need you to respond more like a physician—as someone who wants to help them heal and become a whole person? Name those areas and tell your spouse you will commit to walking alongside him or her with empathy and compassion in those areas of hurt and healing. When everyone is finished, share one or two steps you will take as a couple to express more empathy and compassion toward one another.

Closing Prayer

Take a few moments to pray together in some of the following directions:
- Ask God to forgive each of you for the ways you've questioned your spouse or added to their hurt instead of helping them heal by responding with compassion and empathy.
- Ask God to show you what it really looks like for you and your spouse to heal from past hurts or bad habits and become whole.

- Ask God to give you a new understanding of what it means to be holy and what it looks like to view your marriage as a royal priesthood.
- Thank God for his presence in your lives, for the people in your group, and for the opportunity to be on this journey together as you work toward building a cherishing marriage—even when you or your spouse stumbles.

Between-Sessions Personal Study

SESSION 4

Explore the material you've covered this week by engaging in at least one of the following between-sessions activities. These activities are meant to provide additional opportunities for you and your spouse to climb the staircase from the "ground floor level" of love to the "upstairs level" of cherish. After doing an activity, be sure to reflect and make a few notes in your guide about the experience.

Day One: Physician or Prosecuting Attorney?

Take a few moments to have an honest conversation with your spouse. Ask each other, "Do you feel I treat you like a physician helping you heal or like a prosecuting attorney who constantly reminds you of your faults? How do you want me to respond when you stumble?" Remember, the goal is to listen and stay open to what your spouse is saying. Being dismissive or defensive will only push your spouse away. If needed, take a few moments to write down your answers before sharing them aloud with your spouse.

Read **James 3:2** together as a couple and make it your prayer today: *Lord, we acknowledge we both stumble in many ways. We acknowledge neither of us is perfect, and we are both at fault more than we like to admit. Help us to be aware of the expectations we place on each other to be perfect. Please give us greater grace as a couple— grace that comes only from you. Amen.*

Day Two: Compatibility with Your Spouse

Newsflash: You don't have to be perfectly compatible with your spouse! Cherishing your spouse means seeing him or her as a unique individual. Loving your spouse and his or her unique differences allows you to cherish your spouse regardless of how similar you are or how much you agree with one another. A great marriage doesn't depend on compatibility but on how well you tolerate differences and how you react when your spouse stumbles.

Today, rate how well you respond when your spouse disagrees with you or when your spouse's opinion differs from your own. Now ask your spouse what rating he or she would give you on these times of disagreements. Is it possible you are treating your disagreements or differences of opinion as though they were sin? Write down a few areas in your life where you and your spouse have unique and different perspectives or preferences. Talk about a few ways you could start building a great marriage by celebrating these unique differences.

Read **Ephesians 4:1–3** as a couple and make it your prayer today: *God, please help us to be humble, gentle, patient, and loving with one another. Help us to celebrate our uniqueness, tolerate our differences, respond gently to sin, and, in doing so, let peace reign in our marriage. Amen.*

If you want to build a marriage in which you keep cherishing each other, you have to get over the hurdle of expecting your spouse to be perfect.

CHERISH, PAGE 153

Day Three: Cherishing Your Spouse's Character

During this week's teaching, you saw that in order to cherish your spouse, you have to (1) recognize your spouse may have annoying tendencies that won't change (so you need to let them go), and (2) recognize your spouse will occasionally sin out of his or her own wounded heart (because he or she isn't perfect). Another component involved in cherishing your spouse is to believe that your spouse is a person of character at his or her core—and that he or she is not intentionally trying to hurt you through his or her words and actions.

Today, think about some of the small things that bother you about your spouse and how you have let these small annoyances get in the way of cherishing him or her. Now take a few moments to reflect on the character qualities you admire most about your spouse, and share these with your spouse instead. Because of what you know to be true about his or her character, make a commitment to give your spouse the benefit of the doubt in the future when arguments or differences of opinion arise. (Sometimes, our spouse will truly be guilty, and it's not wrong to call him or her to account. Giving our spouse the *initial* benefit of the doubt is an exercise to seek understanding and facilitate communication, not a long-standing promise to ignore the truth.)

Read **Colossians 3:12–13** as a couple and make it your prayer today: *God, thank you for the gift of being called your chosen people. Help us to respond to each other and to the world around us with love and compassion, kindness and humility, gentleness and patience. Give us grace to bear with each other and forgive one another. Amen.*

Day Four: Cherishing with Maturity

Building a great marriage means cherishing your spouse even when he or she does or says something you consider stupid. It means responding with maturity in those moments—with humility, patience, and gentleness. It means resisting the temptation to view yourself as better than your spouse and remembering that you also say and do stupid things at times. Responding with maturity means *asking questions* instead of *making accusations.*

Today, think of a recent scenario in your marriage when your spouse said or did something you considered stupid. How did you respond? How did your spouse feel as a result of the way you responded? If you're unsure, ask your spouse. Next, consider how that situation might have changed if you had started by asking, "Tell me what you were thinking"? Write down a few thoughts on how you wish your spouse would respond to you when you do something stupid in the future (because, let's face it—we will *all* do something stupid at some point), and then share those thoughts with your spouse.

Read **Proverbs 19:11** as a couple and make it your prayer today: *God, please help us to respond to one another with wisdom, maturity, and patience. Help us to see the glory that comes from overlooking each other's offenses as we build a cherishing marriage. Amen.*

> Cherishing means we don't allow our spouse's
> stumbling to create distance, but rather we
> intentionally craft a generous, gentle, and kind
> response that builds appreciation and intimacy.

CHERISH, PAGE 164

Day Five: Recognize Your Spouse's Royalty

Cherishing your spouse means learning to recognize his or her royalty. While your spouse most likely has not been crowned king or queen of any castle other than your home, God refers to those who place their trust in him through Jesus Christ as "a chosen people" and "a royal priesthood" (1 Peter 2:9). This means the two of you are royalty in God's kingdom.

You may not always be able to honor your spouse for his or her behavior, but you can always honor your spouse for his or her position as a son or daughter, king or queen, in God's kingdom. So today, consider some ways you could recognize God's royalty in your spouse by treating your husband like a king or your wife like a queen. Also ask yourself: *How have I recently treated my spouse like royalty in this way?* Write down a few thoughts and then share them with your spouse.

Read **Psalm 8:4–5** as a couple and make this your prayer today: *Father, help us to remember that we are royalty in your kingdom and that you are always mindful of us as humans. May we remember that we have been crowned with glory and honor by you, the one and only God. And may we learn to see each other in this light and treat one another in this same way—with your glory and your honor. Amen.*

Further Reflection

If you would like to dig a bit deeper into the idea of how to cherish your spouse, read chapter 10 in the *Cherish* book and reflect on the following questions:

- Which story in this chapter stands out to you most? Why?
- What steps will you take this week to extend grace to your spouse when he or she stumbles?
- How will you give your spouse the benefit of the doubt and believe the best about his or her character—even when they stumble and sin?

Use the space below to write any key points or questions you want to bring to the next group meeting.

Taking Your Marriage to the Next Level

Every day of marriage, you're
getting on an elevator that's
taking you up or down.

GARY THOMAS

On a terrifying day in 1981, Ronald Reagan, the fortieth president of the United States, was leaving the Washington Hilton Hotel when a would-be assassin sent a "devastator bullet" (designed to explode on impact) into the President's left side. The day after the assassination attempt—when the severity of the hit was fully understood—Nancy Reagan sought spiritual comfort from Donn Moomaw, their pastor in California. They were joined at a White House meeting by Frank Sinatra and his wife, as well as Billy Graham.

There, in that meeting, Nancy unburdened herself and confessed to the small circle, "I'm really struggling with a feeling of failed responsibility. I usually stand at Ronnie's left side. And that's where he took the bullet." What she was really saying was, *I wish it had hit me instead of him.*

Like the former First Lady, a wife who cherishes her husband wants to protect him. A husband who cherishes his wife wants to put himself in harm's way on her behalf. Cherishing our spouse shapes our mind and heart to such an extent that every cell in our body wants to protect, honor, affirm and take delight in our spouse—regardless of the cost to us. But sometimes this takes hard work *and* an actual rewiring of our brain to begin acting this way.

The latest research in neuroscience shows that our brains are shaped over time by our life experiences. During these experiences, we fashion "grooves" in our brains. These grooves represent repeated behavior that shapes and eventually directs our actions. Over time, these repeated actions become the default mode of response.

Thus, if we want to change the way we respond to our spouse, we actually have to *think* about how to cherish and protect. We have to create new "grooves" by being intentional about how we interact. We have to remind ourselves to think about our spouse with delight. Over time, this will become our natural default mode. We will begin to cherish and protect, to appreciate and affirm, and to take delight in our spouse in new meaningful ways.

Another way of putting this is that the more we cherish our spouse, the more we will cherish our spouse. That is, the actions of cherishing create more feelings of cherishing, which motivates even more actions, which cultivates yet deeper feelings.

Let's get started.

Welcome and Checking In

Begin this session by discussing the following questions as a group:

- What stands out to you from last week's session?
- How have you recently extended grace to your spouse?
- How have you been protected in your life?

Take a few moments to share with the group a time in the past when you felt protected by someone, by something, or by a particular circumstance.

Watch the Video

Play the video segment for session five. As you watch, use the following outline to record any thoughts or concepts that stand out to you.

Notes

We all have "brain fog" moments. Every day of our marriage, we're getting on an elevator that's taking us up or down. Spouses in cherishing marriages look for ways to continually grow closer together instead of letting events—or moments of brain fog—draw them apart.

If we want our spouse to feel
cherished, we may have to
work at a few things we're
not that good at naturally.

There are several steps we can follow to keep pressing the
"up" button to take our marriage to the next level. The
first step is to *protect our spouse*. A couple in a cherishing
marriage will make protecting each other a top priority.

The second step is to *learn to talk to ourselves rather than
listen to ourselves*. Cherishing our spouse means choosing to
hold our tongue in certain situations and instead choosing
to speak to our spouse in a positive way.

The third step is to be *willing to sacrifice on behalf of our
spouse*. There is something about sacrificing that shapes our
hearts and makes the other person more valuable to us.

The fourth step is to *use the power of hugs.* Neurologically, hugging releases oxytocin into our brain—the "cuddle chemical" that promotes feelings of devotion, trust, and bonding. We can use our arms to shape our brains so that cherishing becomes our default response.

> [Hugging] really lays the biological foundation and structure for connecting to other people.
>
> MATT HERTENSTEIN

The fifth step is to *choose our words carefully.* If we want our spouse to feel cherished, we need to use our words as tools to build up the other person instead of tear him or her down.

The sixth step is to *learn to watch and delight.* When our brains grow accustomed to something, we begin to tolerate that thing instead of appreciate it—even if it's something of excellence. We need to consciously step back, watch, and build delight in our spouse so we can have a cherishing marriage.

The final step in building a cherishing marriage is to *conserve our energy*. We can't live with an appropriate intensity for our spouse if we are pouring ourselves out on something else. We have to be ruthless with the pursuits that threaten to take us away from each other.

A cherishing marriage is about continuing to push those "buttons in the elevator" so we can come out to the rooftop and see a cityscape view that takes our breath away.

Cherishing is like the perpetual emotion machine. Once you set it in motion, you keep going higher and higher.

Group Discussion

Take a few minutes with your group members to discuss what you just watched and explore these concepts in Scripture.

1. **Protect our spouse:**
   What is one way your spouse has protected you this week?
   What is one way your spouse could protect you?

2. **Learn to talk to ourselves rather than listen to ourselves and choose our words carefully:**
   Do you choose your words carefully? Why? Why not?
   How can you choose your words more carefully?
   Describe to your spouse how words can make you feel cherished and how words can make you feel demeaned.

3. **Be willing to sacrifice on behalf on behalf of our spouse:**
   How has your spouse sacrificed for you?
   How does your spouse need you to sacrifice for them?

4. Have a volunteer read **Philippians 4:8–9** aloud to the group.
   According to this passage, what does cherishing your spouse look like from a biblical perspective?

5. How have you recently expressed appreciation for your spouse? How has your spouse recently sacrificed for you?

6. Have another volunteer read **Proverbs 18:20–21** aloud to the group. What does this passage say about the way we use our words with each other?

7. Is any area of your life making you so busy or preoccupied that you are failing to cherish your spouse? What is it? Remember, it might be something that sounds "good" (i.e., parenting, volunteering, your job) but that is also distracting you from your first pledge to "love and to cherish." Ask your spouse if he or she thinks anything seems to be taking you away from him or her.

8. Have a final volunteer read **Proverbs 4:20–23** aloud to the group. Why do you think the Bible says to "guard your

heart"? How do you guard your heart and, in doing so, also guard the heart of your spouse?

Group Activity

For this activity, each participant will need a piece of paper and a pen to record ideas.

Part of understanding and exploring what it means to *cherish* one another is to verbalize what it means to appreciate and protect your spouse. You may think, *My spouse already knows I appreciate him or her!* But we all need to hear it from time to time. So take a few minutes to write down a few things you appreciate about your spouse and ways you have felt protected by your spouse, and then share these items with your spouse. When everyone is finished, discuss one or two of your answers as a couple with the group.

Closing Prayer

Take a few moments to pray together in some of the following directions:

- Ask God to allow you to forgive the hurts of the past and even give you the desire to sacrifice for your spouse.
- Ask God to show you what it really looks like to guard your heart and use words as tools to build each other up instead of bring each other down.

- Ask God to help you take delight in your spouse in new ways and to cherish your spouse above all else.
- Thank God for his presence in your lives, for the people in your group, and for the opportunity to be on this journey together as you reach for the "rooftop view" of marriage.

Between-Sessions Personal Study

SESSION 5

Explore the material you've covered this week by engaging in at least one of the following between-sessions activities. These activities are meant to provide additional opportunities for you and your spouse to climb the staircase from the "ground floor level" of love to the "upstairs level" of cherish. After doing an activity, be sure to reflect and make a few notes in your guide about the experience.

Day One: Understanding the Art of Marriage

Take a few moments this week to have an honest conversation with your spouse. Ask him or her, "Do you feel like we're going up or down in our marriage elevator?" If your spouse shares something personal with you, listen and stay open to what he or she is saying. Don't get defensive, as this will only send your elevator to the bottom floor.

Continue by asking your spouse, "What can I do to express more of my appreciation to you? How can I do a better job of protecting you?" Take a few moments to write down something you appreciate about your spouse. You may also want to jot down your thoughts in response to your conversation.

Read **Philippians 4:8** together as a couple and make it your prayer today: *Lord, help us to focus on whatever is true, whatever is noble, whatever is pure, whatever is lovely, whatever is admirable, and whatever is excellent or praiseworthy. Help us to see the best in each other, even when we are at our worst. Deepen our love for you and our love for one another. Amen.*

Day Two: Appreciate and Affirm

Begin this time by sharing with your spouse what you wrote yesterday as it relates to what you appreciate about him or her. Next, consider how you have used your words this week to actually show you appreciate and affirm him or her. Have there been occasions when you used your words to tear down or dishonor your spouse? If so, take this time to seek forgiveness.

Remember that your words are tools you can use to help your spouse feel cherished. Of course, speaking words of appreciation and affirmation may not come naturally at first, and you may have to work at it. You may also have to check your motives and make sure you are not just saying kind words to get what you want from your spouse in other areas of marriage. At a minimum this week, make a commitment to *not speak a bad word about your spouse*. Then extend grace to your spouse as you work toward this marriage goal.

Read **Ephesians 4:29** as a couple and make it your prayer today: *God, we pray that we would not let any unwholesome talk come out of our mouths, especially toward each other. Give us the courage to speak only what is helpful to each other, only the words that build each other up and only the words that benefit each other.*

Be kind and compassionate to one another, forgiving each other, just as in Christ God forgave you.

EPHESIANS 4:32

Day Three: Guarding Your Heart

During the group discussion this week, you explored the idea of "guarding your heart." In marriage, you have the opportunity to guard your own heart and protect your spouse by guarding his or her heart as well. So take a few moments to discuss the following questions with your spouse: *What does it look or feel like for me to protect my spouse? What does it look or feel like for my spouse to protect me by guarding my heart?*

Note that sometimes this conversation can stir up past moments when you haven't protected your spouse or been protected by him or her. So do yourself a favor and just *listen* to your spouse and seek to better *understand* how your spouse wants to be protected. A cherishing marriage is the art of *becoming*. Rather than argue or be resentful about the past, focus on what you can do now and in the future. With that in mind, what can you do to better protect your spouse?

Read **Proverbs 4:23** and **Luke 6:45** as a couple and make these verses your prayer today: *Lord, help us to guard our hearts, knowing that everything else we do flows from it—everything we say, everything we think, every action and step we take—ALL of it is a reflection of our heart. God, we give our hearts to you as individuals and as a couple. We give our words, our lives, and our marriage to you.*

Day Four: The Power of Touch

Take an extra thirty seconds today to give your spouse a big hug, and then consider how you felt during the experience. Did it make you feel more connected to your spouse? Were you uncomfortable? How did you respond to your spouse after the hug? Take a few moments to journal your thoughts below before sharing them with your spouse. Conclude by again writing down something you appreciate about your spouse.

Read **1 John 4:11–12** as a couple and make it your prayer today: *God, we know that you love us so much and command us to love one another. Even though we can't see you with our eyes, we acknowledge that your Spirit lives within us. We acknowledge that your love is made complete in us through Jesus. And we ask that you give us a greater awareness of your love and show us opportunities to make your love known to each other in our marriage. May we grow in our love for one other, knowing our love comes from your deep well of love within us.*

We . . . have to think about *how* to cherish. . . .
We have to remind ourselves to think about
our spouse with delight. It's not *a* choice;
it's a hundred choices, a thousand choices,
and then a hundred thousand choices.

CHERISH, PAGE 169

Day Five: Watch and Delight

Today, think of when you and your spouse were dating. Back then, you couldn't wait to spend time with one other and learn more about each other. You couldn't wait to surprise your would-be spouse with his or her favorites as a way of saying, "Look, I see you! I took notice of the things you love because I love you!" You *watched* and *took delight* in your spouse. Today, write down one thing you could do to take notice of the things your spouse loves, just as you did when you were dating. Then put this into effect during the week.

Read **Isaiah 43:19** as a couple and make this your prayer today: *Father, we thank you that you are making all things new in our lives. Thank you for the grace you give us in spite of our past mistakes and past failures. Thank you that you always make a way for us. Thank you for streams of water when we feel dry and parched. Give us a renewed desire to delight in one another, starting today.*

Further Reflection

If you would like to dig a bit deeper into the idea of how to cherish your spouse, read chapter 11 in the *Cherish* book and reflect on the following questions:

- Which story in this chapter stands out to you most? Why?
- What steps will you take this week to delight in your spouse?
- How can you reorient your schedule to make cherishing your spouse more of a priority?

Use the space below to write any key points or questions you want to bring to the next group meeting.

Keep on Cherishing

The God who cherishes the imperfect
you is more than capable of helping
you cherish an imperfect spouse.

GARY THOMAS

Imperfection seeps into your marriage in more ways than you can count. It can threaten to flood your perspective if you fail to acknowledge one simple fact: *you are as equally imperfect as your spouse.* Your spouse's quirks may make you believe his or her imperfections far outweigh your own, but the reality is neither of you is without flaws. You both have past baggage you have carried into the marriage. You both make bad choices from time to time. And you both are susceptible to the forces of nature as you grow older.

When my friend Greg was a junior medical student in a family practice clinic, he found himself alone in a medical exam room with an elderly couple. The husband seemed spry, energetic, and mentally alert, but his wife sat with a limp body, tilted in a wheelchair. She was expressionless and drooled from her open mouth. Greg felt sorry for this husband, who had to serve as the caregiver for his feeble wife.

Those feelings quickly changed when the elderly man engaged Greg in conversation and told him of his and his wife's past adventures together. Greg said, "For the next ten minutes, I was transfixed as this man—who moments before I had pitied—regaled me with story after story of his life together with his wife. It was incredible. What was more incredible, however, was the change that occurred in me. Gone was any semblance of pity. Instead, in its place was . . . envy." Greg envied the way this older man looked at and talked about his aging wife.

Greg learned that day that youth and physical beauty do not define love, and certainly do not sustain love. Your love for your spouse will be sustained as you take steps each day to cherish him or her over a lifetime together. In time, you will find that person becomes increasingly important to you, because he or she always has been, and always will be. When you cherish your spouse, you build a relationship that stands the test of time.

Let's get started.

Welcome and Checking In

Begin this final session by discussing the following questions as a group:

- What stands out to you from last week's session?
- What is something new you learned about your spouse since session five?
- How have you recently affirmed your spouse?

Take a few moments to share your thoughts with the group.

Watch the Video

Play the video segment for session six. As you watch, use the following outline to record any thoughts or concepts that stand out to you.

Notes

God supplies the power for us to keep cherishing one another. He provides to us his gift of grace, and this allows us to share his grace with others. God's way of cherishing us is through this act of giving us his grace.

Grace is the gasoline that feeds
the engine that drives our
ability to cherish our spouse.

We are all rebellious sinners whom God, through his kindness and generosity, has invited to be reconciled with him. By accepting his grace—provided through the death and resurrection of Jesus—we are saved from God's righteous wrath. This is the *gospel* . . . the good news.

Our ability to keep on cherishing an imperfect and ungrateful spouse is dependent on three gospel truths: (1) how much we ourselves have been forgiven, (2) what we've been saved from, and (3) the cost that Christ paid to win our salvation.

> If we don't seek to be recharged
> with the truth of the gospel,
> we will lose the power and
> motivation to cherish our spouse.

It is finished. Jesus died not to motivate us or inspire us, but to save us. We can't earn God's approval, because we've already received that approval through Jesus Christ. God cherished and loved us first, which gives us the ability to cherish our spouse in marriage.

The power to cherish begins with understanding the gospel message of the goodness and lovingkindness of our Savior. Part of understanding this message is that *we no longer live for ourselves.* The gospel reminds us that if God can cherish us and delight in us as rebellious sinners, then we can certainly cherish those around us.

When we accept the gospel and live it out, we are (1) ready and devoted to doing every good work, (2) are gentle toward the faults of others (as God has been gentle toward us), and (3) are always willing to show courtesy to others.

When we understand how God cherishes us, it launches us into the pursuit of doing good works for our spouse— not to "earn" God's favor but to share the grace that he has extended to us.

Cherishing changes our hearts toward our spouse. It motivates us to actively look for ways to receive God's kindness and goodness so we can bless our spouse with the overflow.

Cherishing is all about plugging into the ongoing power of the gospel so we can treat others gently and actively pursue good works to bless our spouse.

Claim the life of being loved
and loving. Preach the gospel
to yourself every day and then
live it out every moment. That's
the power behind cherish.

Cherish, page 223

Group Discussion

Take a few minutes with your group members to discuss what you just watched and explore these concepts in Scripture.

1. Before everyone shares in the large group, turn to one or two people next to you and finish this sentence: "After watching the video, one question I now have is . . ."

2. What stands out to you from the video teaching: a story, a quote, a thought, an idea? How can you identify with the story of Julie and Jeff in the teaching?

3. How has your family of origin or early background shaped your view of the way God loves you? How has this view positively or negatively affected your relationship with God and those around you?

4. Have two volunteers read **Titus 3:1–8** aloud to the group. How does God's grace change your life?

5. What are a few practical ways you can show kindness and love to one another, your spouse as well as your community?

6. Ask two other volunteers to read **2 Corinthians 5:15–21** aloud to the group. What does this passage mean to you in regard to understanding the gospel message and receiving the power to cherish?

7. What does it mean that you have to worship God before you can work for God? What does this look like—or what *could* this look like—in your life?

8. As a group, read aloud **Ephesians 5:18–20**. (It's okay if you don't all have the same Bible translation.) What does it mean to be *filled with the Spirit*? What does it look like to live this way in community and in your marriages?

Group Activity

For this activity, each participant will need a piece of paper and a pen to record ideas.

The goal of a cherishing marriage is to understand that the call to cherish your spouse begins with understanding that you are cherished by God. Through Jesus Christ, you receive the power to *be* cherished and you receive the power to then *cherish* others. This understanding not only affects your view of marriage but also your view of the people in community around you.

So today, in this closing session, take a few minutes to think about the ways God cherishes you. In what ways have you felt most cherished by God? In what ways have you ignored how God cherishes you? How has your view of the way God cherishes you affected the way you cherish the people in your world?

Take a few moments in quiet prayer and ask God to show you areas in life in which your view of him has affected your view of others. Next, consider how *from this day forward* you will commit to cherishing your spouse. Share your answers with your spouse, and when everyone is finished, share one or two thoughts with the group. Listening to each other and understanding where you've all come from as individuals will enhance the way you cherish one another as you move forward in your marriages and as a community.

Closing Prayer

Take a few moments to pray together in some of the following directions:

- Ask God to forgive you for the ways you've used past experiences to hinder or block your view of his lovingkindness—the way he cherishes you.
- Ask God to show you what it really looks like for you to be cherished by him.
- Ask God to give you a new understanding of what it means to be filled with the Spirit as you interact with the people around you.
- Thank God for his presence in your life and for the opportunity he provides to change your marriage by actively cherishing your spouse.

Personal Study for the Coming Days

SESSION 6

Y ou are invited to explore the material you've covered this week by engaging in at least one of the following activities. These activities are meant to provide additional opportunities for you and your spouse to climb the staircase from the "ground floor level" of love to the "upstairs level" of cherish. After doing an activity, be sure to reflect and make a few notes in your guide about the experience.

Day One: Influenced by Your Past?

Take a few moments to have an honest conversation with your spouse. Ask each other, "Do you think I allow my past to influence my view of God's love for me? If so, how? Do you feel that I allow my past to influence the way I love and cherish you as my spouse? If so, how?" As always, remember that the goal is to listen and understand one another, so hold off on stating personal opinions. Take turns asking each other these questions. If needed, take a few moments to write down your answers before sharing them out loud with your spouse.

Read **1 John 4:19** together as a couple and make it your prayer today: *Lord, we acknowledge that we are able to love each other because you first loved us. In your love there is no fear, no punishment, and no need for approval. Your love is simply love. Help us to fully grasp your love for us as we love each other. Amen.*

Day Two: The Power of Grace

Grace is the gasoline that feeds the engine that drives your ability to cherish. When you accept God's grace in your life, his grace runs through your veins, giving you the blood, oxygen, and energy to love others. This means you don't have to rely on your *own power* to change the way you respond to your spouse, for God gives this power to you—and this changes your marriage.

Today, consider how this truth changes your perspective. How can you rely more on God's power to love and cherish your spouse? Have there been times when you sensed God giving you extra grace and extra love in the way you responded to your spouse? Write down a few areas in your marriage in which you need the power of God's grace to love and cherish one another. Talk about these areas with your spouse.

Read **Ephesians 2:8–10** as a couple and make it your prayer today: *God, thank you for saving us with your grace. Help us understand this gift is not a reward for the good things we've done—it is* *truly a free gift from you. We are your masterpieces, your workman-ship. We have been made new by you so that we can do the good things you've planned for us, powered by your love and grace. Amen.*

Grace is so foreign to us, so supernatural, so
seemingly against logic, that it's not until we
receive it from God that we can give it to others.

CHERISH, PAGE 210

Day Three: A Gospel Marriage

In Titus 3, the apostle Paul paints a picture of what cherishing looks like from a biblical perspective. When you have a mind-set of cherishing others, you are *ready for every good work, speak evil of no one, avoid quarreling, are gentle, and show courtesy to everyone.* On the other hand, cherishing does not involve *acting foolishly, being disobedient, allowing yourself to be led astray, being a slave to passions and pleasures, passing your days in malice and envy,* or *hating one another.* Take a few minutes to quietly reflect on these descriptions, and then confess to your spouse the ways in which you have not been cherishing. Conclude by answering this question as a couple: "What do we want God, our family, and the people around us to say about our marriage?" Make a list of the attributes you *want* to define your marriage.

Read **Titus 3:4–5** as a couple and make it your prayer today: *God, thank you for your love and kindness. Thank you for saving us because of your mercy—not because of anything we've done to earn salvation. Help up to truly live as though our sins have been washed away and we have been made new by you. Help us understand what it means to walk in this new life with the Holy Spirit as our guide. Amen.*

Day Four: Cherishing with God

Cherishing your spouse means learning to cherish him or her *with* God. Cherishing in this way means reminding yourself of God's goodness to you. It means spending time with God so you can be renewed by his Holy Spirit, which in turn will enable you to forgive one another, love one another, and look for ways to bless one another. It's as simple and as powerful as this: *preach the gospel to yourself, and then live out the gospel.*

The truth is that you and your spouse will both fail at this at times. But there's *always* grace—grace for you, and grace for you to extend to your spouse. So take a few moments to think about how will you "preach the gospel" to yourself. What does this look like for you? How will you extend grace to your spouse when he or she fails you? Share your thoughts with each other.

Read **Colossians 4:6** as a couple and make it your prayer today: *God, please help our conversation to always be full of grace and tastefully seasoned with salt. Give us your words to speak so we may know how to answer each other as we learn to cherish one another. Amen.*

Day Five: Cherishing *Cherish*

You develop the art of "cherishing *cherish*" in your marriage when you learn to focus on the positive. The goal of cherishing your spouse is to look for ways to care for your spouse, devote yourselves to loving one another, and do good works for one another. If your focus is only on not doing bad works, then cherishing your spouse becomes about preserving yourself in the marriage. It becomes more about you not making the "wrong" decisions and less about you loving and cherishing your spouse.

Today, consider how you have made this idea of cherishing more about you and less about your spouse. How would your spouse answer this question for you? Pause and ask him or her. Close out the conversation by answering these questions together: "What are some practical steps we could take to focus on cherishing *cherish* in our marriage? What are some steps—some 'good works'—we could take to truly start cherishing one another?"

Read **Galatians 6:9** as a couple and make this your prayer today: *Father, helps us to not become weary in doing good toward each other as we seek to build a cherishing marriage. We know that we will reap the benefits of a cherishing marriage if we do not give up. Give us the courage to keep cherishing cherish in our marriage. Amen.*

Further Reflection

If you would like to dig a bit deeper into the idea of how to cherish your spouse, read chapter 13 in the *Cherish* book and reflect on the following questions:

- What stands out to you most in this chapter? Why?
- What are the three basic gospel truths we can cling to as we understand what it means to cherish and be cherished by God?
- How has God served, loved, and cherished you? How will you seek to serve, love, and cherish your spouse?

That's the power to cherish—believing and
receiving the gospel in which we are cherished
beyond all measure and then living out
the implications to cherish each other.

CHERISH, PAGE 220

Additional Resources for Group Leaders

If you are reading this, you have probably agreed to lead a *Cherish* group study. Thank you! What you have chosen to do is important, and much good fruit can come from studies such as this one. Thanks again for sharing your time and talent.

Cherish is a six-session study built around video content and small group interaction. That's where you come in. As the group leader, you are invited to see yourself as the host of a dinner party. Your job is to take care of your guests by managing all the behind-the-scenes details so that when everyone finally arrives, they can just enjoy each other.

As the group leader, your role is not to answer all the questions or re-teach the content—the video, book, and study guide will do most of that work. Your job is to guide the experience and cultivate your small group into a kind of teaching community. This will make it a place to process, question, and reflect, not receive more instruction.

As such, make sure everyone in the group gets a copy of the study guide. Group members should feel free to write in their guide and bring it with them every week. This will keep everyone on the same page and help the process run more smoothly. Likewise, encourage each participant (or couple) to get a copy of the *Cherish* book so they can complete the suggested readings in the between-sessions study sections should they desire. If this is not possible, see if anyone from the group is willing to donate an extra copy or two for sharing.

Hospitality

As group leader, you will want to create an environment conducive to sharing and learning. For this reason, a church sanctuary or formal classroom may not be ideal for this kind of meeting, as these venues can feel formal and less intimate. Whatever location you choose, make sure there is enough comfortable seating for everyone and, if possible, arrange the seats in a semicircle so everyone can see the video easily. This will make transition between the video and group conversation more efficient and natural.

Try to get to the meeting site early so you can greet participants as they arrive. Simple refreshments create a welcoming atmosphere and can be a wonderful addition to a group study evening. If you do serve food, try to take into account any food allergies or dietary restrictions your group may have. Also, if you meet in a home, you will want to find out if the house has pets (in case there are any allergies) and even consider offering childcare to couples with children who want to attend. Finally, be sure your media technology is working properly. Managing these details up front will make the rest of your group experience flow effectively and provide a welcoming space in which to engage the content of *Cherish*.

Leading Your Group

Once everyone has arrived, it will be time to begin the group. If you are new to leading a small group, what follows are some simple tips you can use to make your group time healthy, enjoyable, and effective.

First, consider beginning the meeting with a brief prayer. Once this has concluded, remind people in your group to silence and put away their mobile phones. This is a way to say "yes" to being present to each other and to God.

Next, invite someone to read the session's "Welcome and Checking In" from the study guide. This will get everyone on the same page regarding that weeks' content. Remember at this point that your role is only to open up conversation by using the instructions provided and by inviting the group into authentic discussion.

Now that the group is fully engaged, it is time to watch the video. The content of each session in *Cherish* is inspiring and challenging, so make sure you leave enough time for personal reflection before anyone is asked to respond. Don't skip over this part. Internal processors will need the more intimate space to sort through their thoughts and questions, and it will make the group discussion time more fruitful.

During the group discussion, encourage everyone in the group to participate, but make sure that if anyone does not want to share (especially as the questions become more personal), that person knows he or she does not have to do so. As the discussion progresses, follow up with comments such as, "Tell me more about that" or "Why did you answer the way you did?"

This will allow participants to deepen their reflections and will invite meaningful sharing in a nonthreatening way.

You have been given multiple questions to use in each session. You do not have to use them all or follow them in order. Feel free to pick and choose questions based on either the needs of your group or how the conversation is flowing. Also, don't be afraid of silence. Offering a question and allowing up to thirty seconds of silence is okay. It allows people space to think about how they want to respond and also gives them time to do so.

As group leader, you are the boundary keeper for your group. Do not let anyone (yourself included) dominate the group time. Keep an eye out for group members who might be tempted to "attack" folks they disagree with or try and "fix" those having struggles (especially spouses). These kinds of behaviors can derail a group's momentum, so they need to be shut down. Model "active listening" and encourage everyone in your group to do the same. This will make your group time a safe space and foster the kind of community that God can use to change people.

The group discussion time leads to the final and most dynamic part of this study: the "Group Activity." During this section, participants are invited to transform what they have learned into practical action. Take time to read over each session's Group Activity segment and make sure you have pens and paper available for the group members. Reading ahead will give you a better sense of how to lead your group through these experiences.

Finally, even though there are "Closing Prayer" instructions for how to conclude each session, feel free to strike out on your own. Just make sure you do something intentional to mark the end of the meeting. It may also be helpful to take time before or after the closing prayer to go over that week's Between-Sessions Personal Study. This will allow couples to consider what they would like to try or ask any questions they have so everyone can depart in confidence.

Debriefing the Between-Sessions Materials

Each week, there is between-sessions work where the couples are invited to choose one or more of five daily exercises. Your job at the beginning of the current week's session is to help the couples debrief the previous week's experience. This time is called "Welcome and Checking In."

Debriefing something like this is a bit different than responding to questions based on the video, because the content comes from the participants' real lives. The basic experiences that you want the group to reflect on are:

- What was the best thing about the activity?
- What was the hardest thing about the activity?
- What did you learn about yourself in the process?
- What did you learn about God from the activity?

There are specific debriefing questions written to help process each activity; however, the aforementioned areas are what the "Checking In" time is designed to explore. Feel free to direct it accordingly. And may God bless you as you lead your group!

Contacting Gary

Although Gary enjoys hearing from readers, it is neither prudent nor possible for him to offer counsel via email, mail, Facebook, or other social media. Thanks for your understanding.

Website:
www.garythomas.com
Blog:
www.garythomas.com/blog
Twitter:
@garyLthomas
Facebook
www.facebook.com/authorgarythomas

To book Gary for a speaking event, please contact him through his website or email alli@garythomas.com.

Cherish

The One Word That Changes Everything for Your Marriage

Gary Thomas

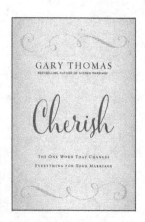

"Most marriages survive by gritting teeth and holding on. But marriages can and will not only survive but thrive when husbands and wives learn to cherish one another."

Those are the powerful words of bestselling author Gary Thomas in his newest book—*Cherish*. And in a world desperate for marriage redemption, it is needed now more than ever.

Thomas shows that although there are a countless number of marriages consisting of two people just going through the motions, there are real ways this pattern can be reversed: when husbands and wives learn to cherish one another in proven, loving, and everyday actions and words.

Through personal stories and real-world examples, Thomas proves what husbands and wives can begin doing today to turn their marriage around—even a marriage marred by neglect and disrespect.

So how do you cherish your spouse? Thomas will show you how going out of your way to notice them, appreciate them, honor them, encourage them, and hold them close to your heart will bring hope, light, and life into your marriage

Available in stores and online!

ZONDERVAN®
.com

Sacred Marriage
Video Bible Study

What If God Designed Marriage to Make Us Holy More Than to Make Us Happy?

Gary Thomas with Kevin and Sherry Harney

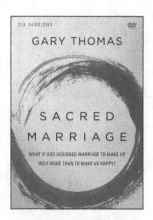

In this six-session small group Bible study, writer and speaker Gary Thomas invites you to see how God can use marriage as a discipline and a motivation to reflect more of the character of Jesus.

Your marriage is much more than a union between you and your spouse. It is a spiritual discipline ideally suited to help you know God more fully and intimately. *Sacred Marriage* shifts the focus from marital enrichment to spiritual enrichment in ways that can help you love your mate more. Whether it is delightful or difficult, your marriage can become a doorway to a closer walk with God.

The DVD features six 10-15 minute live teaching vignettes from Gary Thomas. In addition to life-changing insights, you'll find a wealth of discussion questions in the Participant's Guide that will spark meaningful conversation in your group, between you and your spouse, or to simply ponder by yourself. You'll also find self-assessments, activities, and highlights all created to help you engage deeply and prayerfully with the content of this study.

Sessions include:
1. God's Purpose for Marriage: More Than We Imagine
2. The Refining Power of Marriage
3. The God-Centered Spouse
4. Sacred History
5. Sexual Saints
6. Marriage: The Love Laboratory

Available in stores and online!